I0088498

BITE SIZE
LIFE LESSONS

Modern-Day Proverbs

Volume I

Richard Bartrand

BARTRAND
BOOKS

i

For information about the latest book titles
and to be notified when they come out, log on to;
www.rickbartrand.com/book-titles

CONTENTS

Random, modern-day proverbs
*
Short snippets of useful information
*
Inspirational daily morsels
*
Tidbits of truth
*
One-line treasures
*
Form-fitted advice from experience
*
Things that make you go think
*
A wee bit-o-funnies
*
and some harsh realities

DEDICATION

First and foremost, this book is dedicated to those closest to me that have offered support throughout the process of putting everything together and the patience necessary to accomplish this task. The physical and verbal support was most appreciated and will be remembered forever.

Secondly to all of my friends and fans on all social media platforms that have followed, liked, and commented with positive feedback. That has been instrumental in keeping me going along the way by pushing forward when I didn't feel like doing anything positive at all.

Last but most certainly not least in the lineup are those who didn't even know they helped in any way whatsoever. The ones that gave me inspirational content simply by being themselves, which wasn't necessarily something good, right, or positive but gave me inspiration, none the less because inspiration comes from either wanting to learn what to do or steering away from what not to do.

ACKNOWLEDGMENTS

To a few people that have helped out in the realm of editing the internal layout in regards to spelling, punctuation, and grammar. Lord knows I need a tremendous amount of help in that area.

A special thank you to:

Both my parents, Bernie and Faye for pre-reading. My mother and friend Deb Brode for proofreading, and making the corrections necessary to make this book readable to the public without revealing the fact that spelling was not my favorite subject in school, and giving feedback on what they thought about the content in general.

I am forever grateful for your support and kindness.

Thank You.

PRESCRIPTION

Bite Size Life Lessons

Take daily as needed.

Opportunity Presents Itself

You stand before the closet of choice.

Fear and Boldness hang before you as garments to wrap around and wear this day.

Both are but choices made, constantly shaping your future.

The more you choose one over the other, the more it becomes a part of you as either an excuse to remain in a voluntary prison or a reason to push forward in this conquest we all call LIFE.

Today is the day to take that ragged, torn, and tattered familiar covering of fear and burn it!

Now reach into and take hold of the remaining choice... Boldness... trembling if you have to… but that is only a familiar habitual broken record that has been planted there by your enemy to control you to work in her field of mental slavery.

The redemption papers have been signed long ago, and fear only has a grip on your life by the lingering feeling of shackles around your ankles.

Those feelings are past lies created by your surroundings and those surroundings are nothing more than walls painted with the mindset of an impossible horizon.

Step with courage into your new life of boldness…

One step at a time...

Until that becomes your normal.

~

Your circumstances and the attitude you choose to
display from them, are two separate events.

~

Change failure to opportunity and every opportunity
will be another seed in the garden of your success.

~

Everything is Always about choice... You either have reasons why
you can Or Excuses why you can't.

Choose what matters most.

Good - Bad / Right - Wrong / Positive – Negative...
We all have choices to make every day, all day long.
Be mindful of what you tell yourself. Does it fit inside of who you
want to become or does it keep you locked in an
endless cycle of bitterness and resentment?
Break free now and choose Life.

~

Fear is not a reason; It's an excuse.

~

If deception was belligerent and in-your-face repulsively evil,
it wouldn't be very effective in its profession.
This is proven in modern society by its
incessant drive to call good evil and evil good.
Take a good hard look at your inner workings and be totally
and brutally honest with yourself to reveal your true intentions.

~

You will physically exist in the world you mentally dwell upon.

~

To The Things We Cling

"How are you doing?"

"I'm fine." OR "I'm crappy."

Those two responses are usually based on things such as:

I'm good (because "things" are good)
Or
I'm bad (because "things" are bad).

An Example would go something like this...
Life is good because I'm getting along with everyone in my circle, my car is running good, my bills are paid, or my pet hasn't chewed my belongings into tiny pieces lately.
Or
Life sucks because my spouse is being a #@!%*$!, my car broke down, I got an unexpected bill, I just got dumped, or the weather is horrible.

Question:
Did you know that you can still be "good" or even "joyful," even if everything in your life is going wrong, just by separating yourself from those outside influences?

It's only just a choice away... It's a pretty simple concept.

Choice:
You can either believe it and move past the roller-coaster of emotions by choosing to be good no matter what.
OR
You can continue to be emotionally defined by your physical circumstances.

I wish you the absolute best and hope you make the right choice.

~

Let your obligations be for the truth, not feelings.
Those that "feel" like they have to avoid something
or someone just to save hurting someone's "feelings,"
are more worried about negative conflict
than what needs to be said or done.

In other words, we lie to produce temporary
good feelings in others instead of the truth for hurt feelings.
But that only gives them a false hope
and us true resentment.

It's not a very healthy trade-off
and leads to deeper complications.
The truth may hurt someone's feelings,
but you are not obligated to the way they respond,
only to what you say.

It's also necessary that you make the delivery with
love and compassion behind your words,
but always choose truth over feelings.

~

Your thoughts are not real until you choose to believe them to be.
You are capable of changing your thought process.

~

Life is a gift… Own it…
Everything you do, do it with the conviction
that what you do is already done;
What you want is already yours;
Where you go - Who you are -
What and How you think, do it with all positivity,
integrity, pure moral conviction, and an unstoppable attitude.

~

Pursuing Relationships

When you fight for another person to see things the way you do, you are promoting a negative polarity that naturally repels them, causing them to want to fight for their "right" to return fire by pushing their views back on you.

But...

When you sincerely want to understand the way another person sees things through their eyes, even if you disagree, you are opening up to the positive energy that naturally attracts them, causing them to want to listen to what you want to tell them.

Refocus your aim from a self-propelled message of "you talking," and switch to a goal of "you listening" instead.

Open your mind, accept people for who they are, invite yourself into a new and different point of view, and focus on loving them right where they stand…

You have no idea what they are going through until you climb into their world.

Stop focusing on their differences and separating yourself from them just because they don't believe what you do.

Stop making statements about what you believe and start asking questions and listening to what people have to say, then give it everything inside you to understand why they have come to believe what they do.

This is Love...

Act on it.

~

Thanksgiving…
Add 2 cups of gratitude and
1 heaping smile for a slice of happy pie.

~

Anticipating the worst possible outcome
usually never happens the way we think it will.
So why waste a good thought on something
that won't come true anyway?

Equally as well on the other side of that coin…
nothing ever works out perfectly either.
So, again, anticipating any outcome is a shot in the dark,
which means if you can't predict the future…
and your mind can't help some form of
anticipatory projections for future events…
why not choose the positive outcome over a negative one
and then just accept what turns out as "it just is,"
or "this is what happened, now what?"

Assess the situation and continue forward.
Once you train yourself to manage the better choices…
stress, worries, anxiety, or any other debilitating emotion...
will virtually disappear or, at least, not cause other
negative effects your body will have to deal with.
Win-Win

~

If you look at life through the eyes of your failures,
you will miss what life is trying to teach you.

~

BELIEVE and expect a miracle!!!

~

If you wonder why your life isn't where you would like it to be...
Ask yourself these questions...

1. Who do I hang out with?
2. What do I dwell on throughout the day?
3. What kind of thoughts do I entertain?
4. What do I think of myself?
5. Do I rely on mind-altering substances or non-reality distraction activities to cope with life rather than relying on life itself?
6. How grateful am I?

These are just a few questions to ponder to let the answers speak for themselves. If you're not happy with your answers... think backward.

Answer the questions in a manner of what YOU would like them to be, then find out what YOU need to CHANGE to make it happen!

1. Hang out with people who want what's best for you, NOT what temporary feelings can pacify you until morning.
2. Stop dwelling on past issues or future worries, live NOW!
3. Take your thoughts and decide if they are worthy enough to accept into your new life and reject the old worthless ones that keep you down. Just because a thought pops into your mind doesn't mean you have to accept it as yours.
4. Stop putting yourself down, you are just as worthy as whoever you are putting on a pedestal.
5. Walk away from anything that you rely on to keep your mind distracted from living life to its full potential... in pure form, not altered.
6. Practice gratitude every chance you can to start unlocking life as it should be.
7. If you've been putting down this advice and grumbling the whole time you've been reading it... you need this the most...

Trust me; life isn't going to hand you anything you aren't willing to work for. Yes, it's going to take work and yes, you can do this!

~

Be mindful of your thoughts,
they are the rudders that steer you in the direction you will go.

~

Good Morning!
How are you today?

Choice #1
Crappy / Bad / Miserable "Because" of (your circumstances)

Choice #2
Great / Fantastic / Marvelous "In Spite" of (your circumstances)

Learn to separate your attitude from your circumstances
and watch your life transform before your eyes.

~

If you give expecting to get something in return,
you haven't given anything.

It was just a transaction. Generosity expects nothing in return.

~

In the past, I lived in an endless cycle of negativity for a
very long time, only to find out that it was always up to me the whole
time. Pride will keep telling you to put on the
"I don't care" attitude and keep pushing people away.

But don't listen to your ego; it is a liar, it always has been and always
will be! Life was meant to live... "live" is a proactive choice.
Go out and grab life by the horns.

It's a gift, not a handout: go love the gift; it's yours!

~

Narcissists don't recognize that they are narcissists.

That being said,
I'll guarantee that those who read that statement immediately thought of someone else without even considering themselves being in that category.
We all have narcissistic tendencies… every last person on planet earth to some degree is guilty… and, yes, you read that correctly.

The sooner everyone admits that and realizes it in themselves,
the sooner we will all get along better, knowing that we are all imperfect selfish people living in an imperfect world,
and nobody knows everything there is to know about everything,
concluding that you may be wrong on the very things
you are venomously defending right now.

Give up your belief that you are right about everything you believe
and admit to yourself that you could be wrong along with everyone on earth.
This will solve most issues we are all facing right now as far as relational issues are concerned…
People calling names because someone else doesn't believe what you do or trying to make someone feel ashamed or stupid for not agreeing with your views, these are all narcissistic behaviors that are easily remedied by looking at your shortcomings. Change your outlook from being right and defending it to the detriment of relationships, to want understanding by looking at others' points of view and why they came to the conclusion they did.

Division is never the answer.

So if you are defending a political party, religion, ethnicity, color, title, position... etc. as being the right one or the only one… you are a part of the problem of what is wrong with the world today.

Stop the childish bickering about your opinions of how everyone but you should live.

~

Ahhh,

What to do, What to do, What to do?

Oh, yeah!

Solve the world's problems
&
Get to the bottom of the meaning of life.

I'll be right back.

~

Everyone has something to "not like" about someone else... including them towards you.

Instead of avoiding them, find something you do like.
Stop letting the negative side of humanity dictate your agenda.

You can BE confident without FEELING confident.

You can BE brave without FEELING brave.

Let facts override feelings, not the contrary!

You can still be civil and interact with someone that isn't your favorite soul on earth.

Don't fake it; just find something you like or have in common. You don't have to become best friends.

In regards to attending functions, if there are one or two people you don't care for in a crowd and find yourself avoiding the entire crowd... instead; decide to go because of everyone else.

Stop focusing on what's keeping you from doing something and switch to reasons why you should be doing it.

Stand tall and take charge of your life!

Break out of your shell; shells are for crabs and turtles!

Live life...

Don't avoid it.

~

You will be successful in failing
at every goal you do not set.

Read that again.

~

Don't live in the hypothetical, if you do you're
shortchanging yourself. If something is "going wrong" and you start
to worry about what MIGHT happen instead of just living and
enjoying what is happening right now at the moment,
even though it may seem bad to you.
Things have a way of working out in the end.

~

Your FOCUS will be your FUTURE.

~

Your Goals are like stairs...
without them you lack the means to climb to the next level.

~

WARNING
What goes out of your mouth, Comes into your life!
Words have the power to change your reality.
So choose wisely which ones you use.

~

SERIOUSLY

Don't take life so seriously,
have fun, laugh out loud
and be playful,
go out and do something exciting!

~

This is the year for personal inner freedom.

Break free from the cesspool of socially-driven selfishness and generational programming.

The prison of negative thinking causes stress, anxiety, depression, worries, and every other hook in the flesh that holds you back from peace, love, and joy, and surprisingly enough, has absolutely nothing to do with anything outside of your head!

You don't need anything but you and your own mind to be free. Not a better job, a newer car, more money, a spouse that, so called, "makes" you happy... nothing.

The connections between you and your happiness are just a few focused shifts inside your subconscious habitual thinking, which is the "behind the scenes" programming that makes you do what you don't want to do and don't do what you want to do.

Once you discover what is keeping YOU from YOU, the walls will fall, the veil will be removed, your inner Toto will pull back the curtain to reveal the "Great and powerful Oz," a tiny little desperate balding old man that has no more power over your mind any longer... so you can take over and start living again.

Invest in your mind first...

The rest will fall in line.

~

There are fine lines between peace and unrest;
be aware of each to stay in a state of calm.

DON'T CONFUSE:
Opinions for Facts, Lust for Love,
Infatuation for Passion, Worry for Concern,
Complacency for Contentment or A Smile for Happiness.

~

Determine whether or not someone wants you for you,
Or if they want you for what you can do for them.
One obligates the other appreciates.

~

You WILL face pain.
There is pain in staying the same and there is pain in change.
If you don't recognize the time for change,
at one point the pain of staying the same
will surpass the pain of change.
Push past the pain, there is never any growth without it.

~

Where is your heart?
Do you have a heart of condemnation or compassion?
Both yield different results. One stands on the sidelines judging.
The other jumps over the fence to help.

~

Which Brother/Sister are you?
Pride and Humility are siblings that live in the same house.
One demands to prove that they are right;
The other searches out ways to correct their wrongs.

~

LIFE itself is a vehicle...

LIVE is the proactive word choice we make to get in, start it up and drive.

The "Life" part doesn't "give" us anything except our gift to be alive.

It's up to us to take our life and get out of it what we put into it; (Live) and life gives us exactly what we ask for.

If we choose to complain, life will do its best to give us everything it knows to complain about.

But...

If we choose to be thankful, life will do its best to give us everything it knows to be thankful for.

It gives us what we put into it.

If you put an apple seed in the ground, you get an apple tree.

This is the irrefutable law of Sowing and Reaping.

The same as your attitude is the seed and your physical existence being what grows from it.

If your life isn't what you wanted...

You're planting the wrong seeds.

~

You ARE your thoughts.

FIRST...
Be aware of your thoughts because they cause you to dwell.
Dwelling triggers actions, actions produce habits and your habits are
what builds the foundation for your lifestyle or worldview.

Your life is ultimately what you live through your thought life.

~

Not worrying about an issue that needs attention, and avoiding
responsibilities are not the same.
Don't confuse the two.
Worry is clothed in anxiety, but
concern will motivate you to take care of
responsibilities without the anxiety attached to it.

~

Who am I?
No bigger than a credit card... Able to destroy
countries and ruin lives that last for generations...
Change the course of history and have the power of
life and death... Who am I?

I am the Tongue.

~

Prejudice isn't just about a collective color.
It's being against any person
or people group, religion or political affiliation,
a different country or background,
acts, sizes, shapes, occupations, or any other category
to place another human being into your verbal wood chipper.

~

Who Do You Think You Are?

Self-doubt, negative self-talk, a lack of self-confidence, and low self-esteem are all tools that keep us chained inside the prison of fear.
As long as we are bound by those chains, we will continue to reside in that prison.

Although the fear is real, it's also a lie.

A lie can only affect you as long as you believe it.

To escape from this prison, you must first break those chains and to break those chains you must choose to not believe the lies.

It is not what others say or think about you, but what you choose to believe about yourself.

Take one "thing" that you believe negatively about yourself and choose to believe the opposite.

Then fight through the habitual feelings that have rooted themselves in your routine and prove that new "choice," acting on the new belief by taking a step of faith.

Yes, it will be terrifying, but that is the fear fighting against your success.

The voices that say "you can't" are nothing more than an empty echo bouncing off the walls of your self-made prison that will never stop until YOU ignore them and stop believing the lie.

Fear only exists by choice...

Choose to break free.

~

You've heard the saying…
"Loose lips sink ships."
It's in reference to the power of the tongue
and its ability to cause either life or death,
to heal or destroy, or to change history for better or worse.

~

Just because you don't worry or panic
about a seemingly "bad" situation,
doesn't mean you're not concerned
or don't care about what's going on.
It just means your automatic response mechanism has matured
and you are now more in control of your emotions.

~

Fabricated gods, produce fabricated grace.

~

If you are in control and organize your thoughts,
They will inspire new and healthy emotions.
On the other hand, disorganized thoughts
are caused by your uncontrolled emotions.

~

Do you have conversations or arguments?
If you try to get someone else to see things from your point of view,
and they try to do the same to you,
that is a textbook recipe for an argument…
But,
If you try to see things from their point of view
with the desire to understand where they're coming from,
And they also do the same,
that is the textbook recipe for an intellectual conversation.

~

Feed your mind with words of wisdom.

Read a book that will challenge you to get out of your comfort zone, or dig deeper into your thoughts that are keeping you stuck in your life journey.

Rewrite your future with better "more positive" thoughts.

Get away from the news, endless TV. programs that dull your senses, political nonsense and division, arguments of opinion, constantly checking your Facebook status to see if you got any more likes, email, dead-end routines, worry, stress, anxiety, fear, and yes even in the light of everything going on in the media.

Don't fall for the hype that you have to live in a state of fear to survive. Fear will not change anything.

Just live life as it presents itself to you in a more peaceful, trusting atmosphere.

Focus on the good things in your life that make you smile, the positive things that you enjoy doing and thinking about, the people you love spending time with, and trash the negative thoughts and actions that follow them.

Be courageous and live life as if everything is neither good nor bad, that whatever happens, it just is.

Everything always works out for the good anyway, so don't waste your time giving a circumstance power over you by giving it the meaning of "bad."

Learn how to embrace whatever comes into your life as another step to shaping you into a better version of yourself.

Not good or bad... it just is.

~

Live in the Abundance of Life...

Pursue Love, Peace, Joy,
Truth, Gratitude, Compassion,
Forgiveness, Kindness, Understanding,
Patience, Generosity, Grace,
and everything else on that side of the
spectrum like your life depends on it…

Completely abolish the darkness in your
life. Not by focusing on what "negative
things" you need to get rid of,

But

Focus on the "positive things"
with such passion that
the darkness has no more room to exist.

~

Your Destination;

I'm not a big fan of feeling like I'm stuck in "limbo," waiting for "something" to happen for me to feel accomplished or whatever it is I'm waiting for.

But I have realized that life's journey doesn't really have a destination that we will one day arrive at, other than each day being its own destination in and of itself.

So a more productive approach to contemplate is that wherever you find yourself in this life, is right where you are supposed to be, in the place that you are, feeling what you feel, doing what you're doing, experiencing what you are experiencing...

All to shape you into who you were meant to be.

Just take each day and make the best out of what you have and where you're at.

Get rid of the thought that there even IS a destination, because that breeds impatience, anxiety, and stress.

Just shoot for the best version of you every day and live life in each moment the best way you know how.

Yes... keep your vision and life goals clearly defined in your mind, but don't let the thoughts of accomplishing them cloud your everyday journey in the process.

Just live life...

And live it to the fullest capacity possible.

~

Anger...
Is not a personality or trait, it's an influence.
You were not born with anger issues.

~

Thoughts are like guests…
There are welcomed ones and unwelcomed ones.
Keep your brain door locked and only let in
the ones that will love and encourage you.

~

Trying to abolish hatred, prejudice, racism, and judgment…
With hatred, prejudice, racism, and judgment

Is like trying to extinguish a fire with a lit torch.
You only make things worse and the problems are compounded
by spreading exactly what you are trying to erase.

~

Do you rely on Feelings... or Facts?

Navigating through life using feelings
instead of facts as the means for your guidance system,
is like getting on a roller coaster with the intention
of it bringing you to work instead of your car.

~

Life's too short for a bad cup of coffee.

~

Our battles aren't against political bias,
or color, or gender, or any other preference…
They are against the forces of Good and Evil.

~

It's not that the majority of good people don't know that striving for total and unconditional love is necessary for ultimate peace… it's the few that abandon that concept altogether, that are driven by greed and control that poison that way of life.

Stop feeding into the hatred and division that makes it possible for them to flourish and don't turn against those who share the overall vision for life, but don't share your race, religion, politics, or color.

Stop letting your biases be what separate you from your neighbors. Instead, let them expand your outlook on how they (your biases) can be combined with your neighbor for the sake of strengthening the cause that the majority of human beings all share… To live in peace.

Unfortunately, those who are driven by greed and control are the ones making the most noise, planting the seeds of hatred through the indifference of opinions.
Those are the ones you need to wage war against.

Stand up FOR your neighbor… They're the ones that share your way of life.
Stand AGAINST the establishments that want ultimate control for business, political, or religious gain!

It starts and ends with you!
Be aware of spreading your "influenced" opinions from your chosen biased media sources. Unbiased journalism is dead.

If you want to make an educated decision on anything, go straight to the source, without an already preconceived conclusion, without nit-picking or cherry-picking certain words out of context.

Open your mind to the truth no matter where it takes you...

Don't worry about popularity…

Truth isn't a popular thing anymore.

~

Before you do, think, speak, act, or react... First, ask yourself...
Is what I'm doing, thinking, speaking, acting, or reacting,
Promoting either:

1) Division? Or 2) Unity?

If #1... STOP!   If #2... Carry on.

~

The only thing separating courage and cowardice,
is the action taken when faced with a fear:

The Unknown ~ Humiliation ~ Failure
Death ~ Acceptance... etc.

When each steps up to that line,
Courage steps forward.
Cowardice steps backward.

~

Does it make more sense to give
credit to the car for making itself,
or to the creator and manufacturer of that car?

Are you giving thanks and credit
to the universe or to the one that created it?

~

If you want to be in the best possible
relationships you can be in with others...
Start with the relationship you have with yourself.
If you don't care for you, there isn't a single person on earth that
will convince you that they do either.

~

If you want to find your true potential for good, you have to realize the potential of evil in yourself.

Meaning:

Your journey in life sometimes brings you to a false sense of goodness, which in most instances renders as self-righteousness.
And that's not a "good" thing but, it's usually perceived as good, which is the deception of self-righteousness.

Coming from that standpoint to find, what I'll call "actual goodness," you have to abandon all proclamations of self-goodness and come to an inner realization of the depth of absolute evil that you are capable of.

From there, let that realization scare you enough to use every possible asset available to avoid any prompts to entertain any action in that direction, which in turn will render the end result with the characteristics of goodness without the selfish ego attached.

Claiming to be good is an act of the over-inflated ego and foolish on many levels…

So,without that in the way, you aren't necessarily a good person… you're just so appalled by the potential of evil in yourself that you let that realization be the repellent for such acts:

Which crush the self-righteous ego attempts and end up where you want to be, but in a state of humility and not arrogance.

One blinds you into believing you are good.

The other inadvertently achieves it in the deductive sense of the meaning.

~

Stop saying "I'll do it tomorrow"…
Tomorrow will always be one day ahead of you.
Start today, Today is the only day you have to live.

Be honest with yourself… Who's the procrastinator?
Is there something you could do today
that your first thought would be…

I'll do it tomorrow?

~

When your first reaction to any given
adverse circumstance in life is to let your thoughts,
feelings, or emotions dictate your bad mood or negative actions,
you are letting your horses run wild in the field of chaos.

Your mind was designed to be in control of your thoughts,
feelings, and emotions, Not the other way around.
Conquer that task and you will be
exponentially closer to the life you want to live.

~

What is the first thing you do
when you wake up to set the pace for the day?

Conquer your mornings with declarations of;
Love, Joy, Peace, Truth, Honesty, Integrity,
Understanding, Compassion, Humility, Gratitude,
Forgiveness, Grace, Mercy, Freedom, Etc.

~

Sometimes the smile hides a broken heart.
So smile; Someone might need a jump start.

~

Appreciation Has Many Voices

Some appreciate focused time; others, affirmative words.
Some appreciate meaningful gifts and still others appreciate a touch of kindness or affection.

We all speak different languages in that area so if you're speaking the language that you prefer to someone who doesn't share that same language, they neither totally hear nor fully appreciate your attempts to communicate.

For instance:

If someone who understands time spent with them as being important, then your kind words to them won't mean as much as they might mean to you.
Being offended at their lack of expected response from your gesture is like getting upset with someone in a foreign country for not understanding your native language.

To make relationships more effective, find out what they speak…
Then learn to speak it fluently.

The most valuable life lessons we need to learn are hidden in the things our first instincts say to resist.

You can't learn patience, without the things that test it.

You can't learn unconditional love, without those who push your buttons.

Remember…

Iron sharpens Iron.

~

If you are afraid to move out of your comfort zone
and think that you can just wait for something to come to you...
the only thing coming is failure.
You always succeed in failing to try.

~

Nothing great has ever been accomplished in a safe space.
Leave your teddy bear in the comfort zone.

~

When you grasp the fact that your beliefs are what dictate
your life, then you will be able to walk through
many more doors of opportunity.

~

If you believe that you are not good enough... You're not.

If you believe that you are good enough... You are.

Believe it... Live it...

~

If your experience with religion/church is generating
any form of obligation as opposed to appreciation,
then you should re-consider
the position you are committing yourself to.

Never choose religion over God.

Denominational religious institutions
will teach you how to become religious...

God will teach you how to be free.

~

I am not defined by vocation, location, or opinion. I choose to separate myself from where I work, where I live, and the views and judgments of others.

We can all rise above the negative influence of others that tend to pull us down into self-doubt or depression.
We are all a one-of-a-kind creation of the Creator of the Universe,... Who am I, or anybody else, to define differently?

My purpose is to reflect the uniqueness that I was given, in the light of a life that shines bright with Love, Joy, and Mercy that was also extended to me by my eternal Father.

He not only gave me this life to live, but to live it to the fullest extent, not only here on earth but stretching well into the realm of forever.

Stay thirsty my friends, with a thirst for righteousness.

~

Do you want to navigate to respectable places in life and make a difference to feel good about yourself?
Stop finding things to complain about or victim groups to identify with.
Take responsibility for the way you turned out REGARDLESS of who had any influence on your outcome.

Stop feeling sorry for yourself and wallowing in self-pity.
Start focusing on what you CAN do, HAVE done, and the things that DID work out.

EVERYTHING is a choice from this second forward!
EVERYTHING that has happened from the last second backward no longer matters in your existence.
You are NOT a color, religion, sexual preference, a job status, or belong to any ethnicity! You are a human being created to do great things! Make up your mind to do them, then put some actions behind that mindset and get it done.

~

Your attitude is the mirror of your life.
Your reflection is the reality
that stems from your thoughts.

If your life sucks now…
Your thoughts sucked first…

Thoughts = Actions

Actions = Habits

Habits = Your life.

~

Believing to choose the ways of the Source of all life, is not acquired by a human intellectual debate, but by a spiritual transformation acquired by the faith taken from the evidence that surrounds you.

Those who have not been transformed, will believe it to be foolishness…

Those who have been transformed, will believe it to be as evident as life itself…

No one knows everything, so you only mock what you have not yet established as true knowledge, and when that knowledge has been put into practice it becomes wisdom, and when wisdom has been rooted it becomes a way of life so deep that death is now embraced as gain.

Only then will one understand and experience a true transformation.

The more you cling to your own inferior will, the more the source of life gives you over to your own mind.

Think for a moment how much power it took to create the unfathomable universe.
Now think how ridiculous it is to fight against that power.

There is a mercy that will still accept the mocker up to their very last breath, which is not guaranteed past the next one.

～

You were born with a God-given potential that can scale the highest of mountains! You have so much more strength than you think you have and are loved much more than you think you are.

Break the illusionary chains that are hindering your growth and be who you were born to be.

~

TRUTH
The easiest cure, Inside the toughest pill.

Pursue the truth until you find it.
Sometimes the truth isn't what you want to hear,
but it's not going to make it go away simply by ignoring it.

~

Never avoid anything
because you assume something.

~

If you want to be right... You argue.
If you seek understanding... You converse.

To gauge your intentions for a conversational outcome;
if you want to argue - you go in with a closed mind,
but if you want to have an intellectual conversation,
open your mind to understanding where
someone else is coming from.

~

Feelings have some purpose in this life,
but relying on them to dictate the outcome of your day
is not one of them.

Navigating throughout the day with your feelings
dictating your emotional stability
is like letting the waves steer your ship across the ocean.

Grab the rudder wheel and rely on
intentional responsive action, not automatically reacting
out of a triggered habitual program.

~

To Live... Is to Love

Every day, All day, Eat your fruit from the Tree of Life.

The fruits are Love, Joy, Peace, Patience, Truth, Contentment, Kindness, Self Control, Hope, Freedom, Gratitude, Generosity, Humility, Thankfulness, Honesty, Caring, Bravery, Understanding, or anything else Positive, Good, and Righteous.

Make these your Habits and you will find your life worth living...

Anything else that is bad or negative will only take life from you. Avoid them at all costs.

Fight for life.

You were born for greatness, worth, and purpose to live this life to the fullest capacity.

Don't let anyone hold you back or make you feel guilty for your dreams.

If you are down or depressed, you are choosing the fruits that drain life from you. Take your thoughts captive, reject the ones that promote death, and only let the ones through that feed your soul.

Your struggle is not in the material or physical, the things that can be taken from you or lost, like relationships, houses, money... etc. But rather in the mental and spiritual; your thoughts, attitude, and your inner choices to reject the negative influences of life.

Switch your focus and stop letting circumstances dictate your feelings and choose to BE fantastic even when things don't work the way you want them to.

Bite Size

~

It's not that miracles don't happen...
It's that they happen so often and on such a grand scale,
that we take them for granted.

Sometimes things are so obvious
that they are difficult to notice.

The reason we can't see the miracles all around us
is like the comparison to the saying,
"You can't see the forest for the trees."

But as soon as you shift your focus to one tree,
you start to see them all, (the forest)
and in such abundance, you'll wonder
how you could have missed it this whole time.

~

Who will you be this time next year?

Only you have the power to become who you want to become,
do what you want to do, and accomplish
what you set your mind on.

So make up your mind and go...

• • •

When the clock strikes 12 one year from today,
Will you be the new or the old will you stay?

Make a decision right here and right now,
Then start your new journey with the why and the how.

When now turns into your memories of last year,
The answer to this challenge will also be clear.

~

I believe when adversity befalls us, most people's default, when it comes to attitudes, is negative: As if to display our inward feelings of disgust, because life isn't complying with our unrealistic standards of perfection right now.

Think about this… Are you still alive? Has everything up to this point worked out? (Maybe not the way you'd have preferred, but it still worked out?)

Question…

Which would you choose?

Anxiety, stress, worry, anger, fear, and restlessness, all leading to various forms of misery. Or… Rest, contentment, happiness, joy, trust, gratitude, all leading to a deep state of peace?

Notice the question… which would you CHOOSE? Those are all choices that are 100% attainable inside your personal spectrum of reality.

Fact…

Your negative behavior to all adversity was an observed and repeated action that inadvertently led to an automatic habitual reaction that you, without conscious awareness, took on as just being a part of who you are.

But, like any bad habit, it can and will change by first being aware of it, then taking steps to reverse and replace it with a more preferable, intentional response that produces the outcomes on the positive side of that spectrum.

Conclusion…

Instead of automatically reacting negatively because you were taught to before you had a choice, be aware and in control of your behavior by intentionally responding to every situation or circumstance with a well-thought-out and a new habitually-positive reaction to the non-preferable but inevitable adversities in life.

Adversity WILL come, so why not choose the most preferential outcome instead?

~

Challenge your mind to do bigger and better things.
One step at a time.

~

Your relationships are only as good
as your ability to see things through their eyes.
If you truly want to see things from someone else's point of view,
you will try to understand why they say and do what they do.
You'll be surprised at how many arguments you won't get into.

~

You physically live in the world you mentally dwell upon.
Be fully aware of the thoughts you choose to believe
about yourself... If they aren't what you want...
Change them. Then own it!

~

Silence...
Speaks Volumes

~

Don't ever sell yourself to someone else's expectations,
opinions or definitions of who they want you to be.
Their definition of you is only written in their dictionary
and does not transfer to yours by default.
You were defined by your maker and His is the only one that counts.

~

If your heart is ugly...
Your pretty skin isn't going to cover it.

Your outer appearance can change with what your lips
let pass from what lurks in your inner character.

~

Your bank account doesn't determine your worth... Neither does how many likes you get on any given social media post... Or what people call you or think of you... Or how many friends you have or don't have... What you look like... How you act... What you believe in... What size your house is or how new your car is... If you have a house full of people or live alone... What country you were born in... What connections you have or don't have...

Everything can be stripped away from you in a second, so what defines you when you have nothing left but your character?

Do you choose to follow your selfish ambitions to take advantage of, step on and use whomever it takes to get you there or do you practice the less-traveled path of doing the right thing, even when nobody is watching, when you don't feel like it, or when it benefits someone else more than it benefits you?

Look out for Number One? Or Look out for Every One?

~

You will never move past your fears, hurts, etc. until you stop giving them the power to keep you there.
Every time you go over, either verbally or in your head, your past hurts, or your future fears, you are giving them the power to keep you in that prison.

Let go of that power and the bars will disappear. Then you will be able to move on in life.
Most of the time, truth is a hard pill to swallow but trying is an excuse... only DOING will produce results.

Yesterday has a headstone. Tomorrow has yet to be born. Today is a new day! Put your faith to work and go accomplish something other than complaining about your past or worrying about your future. Both ways are completely worthless for a healthy or successful existence.
It's like betting all your money on a dead horse.
You will lose every time.

~

No matter what you say or do, there will always be people
that love you and hate you just for being you. So...
you might as well not care what anybody thinks of you.

That being said... There are those who boast to be
"strong and independent."

They take the "I don't care" attitude in the other direction and it's
nothing more than an, in your face, loud, obnoxious,
belligerent, and self-righteous display of arrogance.
If that's you...

There is a sweet spot in the middle that is called self-confidence
that doesn't care what anybody thinks, but still has the common
decency to have respect for humanity and personal space.

~

You are free to complain about what has happened,
or plan for what will happen.

~

Don't waste your imagination on the past or how things
"could" have been.
Use your memories for the past, but only as a reference to stay away
from the things that didn't work and to improve on the things that did.
Use imagination to build your future and move in that direction
until that also becomes a memory to improve on... Then... Repeat.

~

Your sails will be filled by the wind of your expectations.
If you expect a negative outcome, then prepare to land at the dock of
despair. Throw that map in the trash and command your new
coordinates to ride the jet stream of life and expect the best.

~

I've been alive long enough to know that Maybe pretty much always means No. *(Jack Johnson even wrote a song about it)*.

That... I'm too busy, don't have time, can't afford it, and don't have the money means that it or you aren't a priority.

That intention and reality aren't even in the same ballpark.

That if you are selling something and tell someone it will cost between $300.00 to $500.00... they heard you say $300.00 while you meant $500.00.

That whoever has the upper hand will most likely and selfishly take advantage of that fact.

That you will judge yourself by a very padded, lenient, self-righteous set of standards with plenty of room for error and others with a rigid, thin line, and a much smaller set of standards with very little room for error.

That your definitions of something being full, or in a minute, later, sometime, and pretty much everything else, are NOT the same definitions as the person you are in any relationship with.

This list is extremely long, but the moral of these short stories is that clear communication is paramount in any and every relationship you are involved in.

Let your No be No and your Yes be Yes.

Let your words and actions always line up.

Taking it a step further...
Make sure your intentions are true to both.

Don't say "YES" with your words and follow through with your actions when inside you mean "NO."

~

THINK IT

DO IT

BECOME IT

The blueprint for your future.

~

Picture, if you will...

Something negative happens in your life that you don't prefer to happen…

You automatically label it a "bad" thing.

You subconsciously and habitually react out of anger, fear, stress, anxiety, and start negatively complaining about your circumstance… Too hot, too cold, flat tire, got dumped, whatever happened.

Here's a different thought…

You assess the situation and intentionally respond with… This just happened, now what?

Then move forward by figuring out a solution to your dilemma and positively accepting whatever you can't change and take from it a learning experience.

Ask yourself a question…

Which scenario will end in the most productive and fulfilling experience?

Facts:
You can't change the past… or what has happened to you.

Nothing gets better or changes by complaining about it.

In a Nutshell:
Reacting with any negative emotion to anything that has already happened, or to something you can't change, is like banging your head against a wall and wondering why you have a headache.

~

I believe the secret to successfully maneuvering through this life
is finding the balance between…

Man I just absolutely, beyond comprehension, love this moment
and holy %#@*and)^%$# I wish God would just
violently rip the breath right out of me.

~

Fun Fact.
Did you know...
That hippopotomonstrosesquippedaliophobia
is one of the longest words in the dictionary and the meaning is…

The fear of long words.
Just thought I'd pass that on. Now ya know.

~

A gift isn't measured by how much money you spend,
but by how much of your heart you put into it.

~

You can't experience the true depth
and richness of the things you love,
without the same level of opposition
on the other end of the spectrum to compare it to.

You can't fully experience Good without Evil.
You can't fully experience Love without Hate.
You can't fully experience Light without Darkness.
You can't fully experience Peace without War.

There is a season and reason for everything under the sun.

~

True happiness doesn't hinge on a circumstantial outcome, but more of the attitude in which you take inside of that circumstance...
"Good" or "Bad."
Even those terms are based on our self-defined expectations of preferences or non-preferences.

If you want to change your attitude... change your expectational preferences.
A suggestion would be... to abandon your presupposed judgments of how you think that life should turn out based on the unrealistic expectations that it should always end in the way you prefer, and remain open to everything happening the way it actually does.

In other words, get rid of the terms "good" and "bad" altogether, and now after every circumstance that happens, choose the best course of action forward by saying;

It happened... Now What?

~

If you focus on nothing but your sufferings, that, in and of itself, will cause more suffering.

This will make you believe that your suffering is useless and has no meaning whatsoever, which will also prolong the suffering.

Shift your focus to the reasoning behind your suffering and try to find the purpose in it.
Learn from it, which will release most of the sting and get you to take your eyes off the past, the cause of projected suffering, and place them on the future, the reason for growth, which will ultimately lift you to the next phase of life.

Suffering is real and an essential part of life but it's not without purpose.

~

Never "CHOOSE" to be a victim!
You may have been the recipient of an unfortunate circumstance
but letting that circumstance dictate the outcome of your future
is another "CHOICE" that only you are responsible for.
In other words...
Taking responsibility for the way you respond
to everything in your life, as if your life depended on it,
(and it does)
is far more productive than blaming the "nouns"
for your self-proclaimed, messed up miserable life...
and even that mindset is a choice.

~

Don't think you "NEED" more.
What you need is to "WANT" less.

~

So you think, So you are.

~

Be dangerous enough to **stop** evil
but controlled enough not to **be** evil.

~

Take a deep breath...
It is perfectly OK to be you... Unless of course, you're not.
Don't try to be someone else.

~

We all have scapegoats that we
tend to blame by pointing our fingers;
however, that scapegoat is nothing more than
our own reflection in the skin of someone else.

~

How about we all stop calling ourselves by what color or gender or occupation or political affiliation or religion or ethnicity or social status or weight class or every other thing that even hints at dividing anyone into categories of separation.

Just live life without any judgmental attitudes.
If you want to actually see someone... look into their eyes.
The eyes aren't prejudiced even though they're different colors, the eyes don't gain weight or speak a different language, you can train yourself to see what you want to see.
So if you're seeing your world in dark surroundings... turn on the lights.
Your eyes are the light of your soul.
If you want peace, joy and love in your life, stop judging by what's different about others and see only the similarities.

~

Each and every one of us has the potential for absolute good or absolute evil within our hearts. Both sides are calling us to try just a little bit at a time until either one or the other gains dominance.

Human nature usually keeps us stuck, within marginal variations, right in the middle.
A gray, lukewarm, straddling the fence area that always keeps us waiting or wanting, and not committing to one side or the other.

Most days are spent just automatically reacting to what's next in the lineup and not intentionally driven by any purpose at all. Live for purpose; fight your way out of the gray areas of life; be intentionally good, positive, find things to be thankful for! Break free from complacency and live!

If you don't know how... ask someone whose life reflects true deep happiness and contentment.

P.S. Be cautious of masks...
There are a lot of posers out there.

~

Stop asking yourself what's wrong with you…
but, rather, ask what is right with you.

~

Be skeptical, but don't let it be a reason to keep
you from believing something.

Let it be the reason you search to uncover
a truth you've been playing ping pong with.

Skepticism is healthy,
unless you let it stop you from pursuing
what it has yielded you from in the first place.

Consider it a challenge instead of an impenetrable wall.
Either find a way through or over it,
but keep from camping at the bottom of it.

~

You're stronger than you think... You're still here, aren't you!

~

Einstein once said that everyone is a genius,
but if you judge a fish by its ability to climb a tree,
it will believe it's stupid for the rest of it's life…

Do you believe you're stupid or not enough or you just don't fit in?
To whom or by what standards are you comparing yourself?

Tell yourself that maybe you are just supposed to be You
and not anyone else.
Then start comparing yourself to who You want to be
and swim in your own ocean... and start today.

~

Every day gives us lessons to learn.

Things to do over or never do again.

Places to go again, or never go back to.

The thoughts that are worthless to dwell on and the ones that will carry you through.

The people you can trust every word they say and those you can't trust anything they say, with every variation in between.

The nouns that are worth your limited time and the ones that aren't worth one more second.

Let all your experiences in life add to and subtract from your future to funnel down into the life you choose to live.
Keep returning to the people, places and thoughts that fill your tank with the things that you can then fill others with, that keep returning to you.

This means that you have to BE that person to others.

Be filled for the purpose of filling others and the more you fill others with the best version of you, the more you will be filled.

Just keep the refining process going until you find your dwelling space.

Then live it with every ounce of life you have in you.

~

Life takes work...
So does baking cookies, but look what you get from that.

The moral of the story...
If you give up, you don't get any cookies.

It might be hard now, but keep adding the ingredients:
4 cups of You can do this, 1 gallon of You Rock,
A pinch of Breathe Deep and let it out slowly,
Determination, Keep your eyes on the goal, and
See it through until the end... then...
Eat Some Cookies

~

Get rid of your assumptions and expectations
and about 90% of your frustrations will mysteriously disappear.

~

Sometimes we need the cold hard truth
and not the padded, watered-down version of reality.

When the fluffy feel-good stuff keeps us stuck in a holding pattern
of complacency and feeling sorry for ourselves, it has absolutely no
value at all in our growth.
It only temporarily gets us through another day.

If you want to move past the band-aids
and dig the roots out for permanent change,
seek out the painful, deep issues that will reveal
what is necessary for true and lasting strength and peace.

Don't seek what you already want to believe,...
seek truth at all costs.

~

The Existence of the Source of All Life is not up for debate.

The conscience alone should prove that there is another invisible dimension that guides us in the right direction and gives us the check system against wrong decisions that will bring us harm.

But the selfish ego will try to fight those promptings with resistance, due to the pride of life and the lust of our one-sided desires for a "I'm the only one that matters," attitude.

This battle is the realm of good and evil, defined as an influence or a force that pulls us in either direction to dominate our thoughts.

Our thoughts transition into actions and our actions eventually develop into habits and ultimately into a lifestyle.

The way you are living right now first started as a thought, whether it was originally yours or inadvertently influenced by someone else or collectively by a group of peers.

Thoughts can be changed, which means that lifestyles can be changed. So if you're at odds with life... proven by the fact that you're not living in a state of perpetual peace, love, and joy...
You are fighting against an irrefutable law of nature that was instilled at birth and written on the tablet of your heart.

You come complete with a God-given guidance system called the conscience...

Use It!

~

When you are out of balance,

Return to the Source.

~

Control

In reference to the need for external control,

To varying degrees, is one of the major causes of most issues that, I see, people face on a day-to-day basis.

The black-and-white truth is: if you get upset or offended over what others say or do... You have control issues. Straight and to the point.

An example of giving up control is:

If you allow others to say and do what they say and do without reacting negatively or taking anything personally.

Also meaning that you can have an intellectual conversation with those who you disagree with, even if it's on every subject, and remain calm and in control of your own emotions and reactions without trying to force them to believe your views or getting upset when they don't.

Work on the maturity in yourself, so You WON'T be offended, more than working on getting others to believe your opinions, so that you DON'T get offended.

Please read that as many times as necessary to understand the meaning.

Let go of "external" control... circumstances, situations, others opinions or beliefs... and rather work on "internal" control... your thoughts, actions, and reactions...

You can only control from your forehead inward...

Not from your forehead outward.

~

If you woke every morning and just did one thing
that you know you should do to change for the better,
who would you be in one year?

~

The more you care what people think of you,
the less you live your life.

~

Don't be afraid of doubt,
because it's through doubt that we come to believe...

With your whole heart, keep asking, seeking,
and knocking, my friends, and you will find the truth.

~

CONTROL
is not Your friend! Give it up and live in peace.

~

You are servant only to what you fear.

~

Doubt isn't a stop sign, it's a yield sign!!!

~

If your feelings are telling you to be sad, unhappy, anxious,
stressed, discontented, etc.,
Tell them to pack their bags and evict them from your
head house and replace them with new tenants such as
love, joy, peace, patience, contentment, etc.

Live by intentional faith, not by reactionary feelings.

~

A Letter from humanity to the whole human race.

I come with strong points and weak,
I have good in me and bad,
I love life, but hate parts of it.

If you want only the good side of me without the bad,
then you really don't want me at all.
I am a complete package,
so if you love me for what I can give you,
but don't want any part of my flaws,
then you really don't love me either…

I can't put it any other way.

Life has a melting pot of emotions and feelings,
joy and pain, excitement and disappointment…

Take one… and Take it all.

This is not a place to cherry-pick the best
and disregard the rest.
That would be an arena of deception
and unrealistic expectations.

So If you think life is all about YOU,
I have no room for your thoughts,
because mine make room for the full spectrum
of who you are…
with me… and who I am!

Together…

As one beautiful mess to another.

~

If you rely on a substance to alter your reality,
then you can also be controlled by that substance.

~

Faith = I'll cross that bridge when I get there!
Failure = "What if" there is no bridge when I get there.

When you live life in the hypothetical realm, it keeps you
from taking the first step, and if you don't take the first step
every one after that is a guaranteed failure.

The Point!
Don't worry about the obstacles,
Make them a part of the journey.

Whatever is holding you back is an Excuse.

If you want something in this hand,
you have to let go of something in the other.

If you let go of the "T," CAN'T changes to CAN!

~

If your pursuit is to uncover the absolute truth…
Your path will undoubtedly keep company with much solitude…

~

Watch it happen, Or Make it happen.

~

HEY!
If you're reading this, You are special.
and loved far beyond what you know.

~

The Human Mind is the most powerful asset in the toolbox of life. Be cautious of what you put into it, because it's what you pull from to build your experiences in this existence.

What you believe is what you live.

Your focus is your future.

Everyone is heavily influenced by the world's system of selfishness. AKA, The Matrix. It's up to you to seek out a higher way of thinking and living that will cause you to rise above this system and live according to the original divine design that was put into motion by the One who created life itself.

There are a series of spectrums that dictate what plain of life you reside in... For instance...

The spectrums of Good and Evil, Right and Wrong, Positive and Negative, Love and Hate, Sad and Happy... etc.

Each side of those influences has a choice attached to it and can be changed every step of the way.

As long as you have blood running through your veins and breath in your lungs... you have the power to choose one over the other no matter what circumstance is attached to it.

As soon as you can grasp the absolute power you have over every situation, circumstance, occurrence, thought, action, reaction, feeling, emotion, etc. you will be unplugged from that Matrix, to climb out and start living above that cesspool.

This concept goes way deeper than just these few words you see here in front of you, so I encourage you to dig your heels in and prepare yourself for a journey that will challenge you to pick up your old habits, thoughts, and life, to toss them in the trash and never look back again.

~

You can be one of two kinds of people...

1) The Voice of Encouragement
Pointing out someones strengths, the positive and good
accomplishments that they have done to motivate them
to continue down that path.
Or
2) The Voice of Discouragement
Pointing out their faults, the negative and bad things that
they have done to cause insecurities, and a lack of motivation to
continue, especially in children growing up.

Of course, there is constructive criticism but that is reserved
for a delivery out of love and compassion,
not a direct harsh jab, out of your own insecurities or
to sound superior in your inflated egotistical wisdom.
Rather, come from a place of understanding and if you
have constructive criticism, make sure you have already
evened it out with plenty of positive feedback.

~

In the kitchen, in the wood shop, in the music studio...
in the process, you make a mess on the way to a masterpiece.

So if you're an absolute mess right now...
awesome; that just means you are in the process
to become a masterpiece.

Trust the process!

~

Just "DO" Love!
No one can take that from you.

~

If anyone has been alive long enough to be able to read this, you can conclude that we all have experienced various kinds of heartaches, pain, trauma, betrayal, and everything else on the bottom side of the spectrum of good and bad.

Everyone struggles with something and struggling is a part of learning, learning is a part of growing, and growing is a part of life.

So be patient with everyone and just know you're not alone. Some have made it past the struggle that you're in now. Reach out to them, it's OK to ask for help and it does not mean you're weak.

Never tell yourself that you are too far gone! That is an enormous lie! No matter where you are in life, some answers can navigate you through it. You just might not know what they are yet, hang on to hope and never give up. You will make it.

~

If you have regrets, you're living in yesterday!
If you have worries, you're living in tomorrow!
Live in today with its adventures and challenges!

Enjoy the here and now with love and acceptance. Breathe deep with contentment and let your eyes only see the things that are positive, good, and right.
Develop blindness for prejudices of all things alive and strive for a prosperous existence: Not a materialistic prosperity but an emotional one.
Fill your storage barns with love, joy, peace, contentment, patience, and the things that thieves can't take from you:

The true and lasting prosperity that is free and meant for everyone to live out this life to the fullest possible meaning of living life, not just existing in a hopeless, empty, hole that focusing on material gain offers you.
Yesterday is gone. Tomorrow doesn't exist...
LIVE NOW! With what you have... Now.

~

If you don't take control of your mind, that generates your feelings
and emotions, then they will take control of you.

If you are consumed by past traumas, circumstances,
bad relationships, etc. and are projecting them into the future,
you will assume that your future is doomed and you are
turning into a hopeless mess.

But it is not the future "you" that is a mess...
It's the false projection of the future "you"
because the past is blinding your potential.

Letting go of the past will clear your vision
so you can project a happy, healthy you
and from there all you have to do is
step into the new "you".

~

Tomorrow is a new day full of new
beginnings and new opportunities.

Let today and all of its disappointments and mistakes
fade like a vapor of smoke in the wind.
Don't carry them into your future.
Tomorrow is a new day.

~

The thoughts you invite into your mind for coffee,
will eventually be the residents
that move into your house of reality.

~

GOOD minus GOD = O

~

NOTHING CAN MAKE YOU MAD!

It is your choice to let circumstances dictate your emotional well-being.
What has already happened, has happened... It does not change facts when you get angry, it just changes your energy from positive to negative.

Let go of things you cannot change and choose to either fix what went wrong or move on.
You can accomplish both with a positive attitude and a joyful disposition.

Pluck your fruit from the Tree of Life.

~

It sickens and saddens my heart at the same time for those who choose to deceive and the ones that fall prey to their deception.

If you're not pursuing the truth at all costs, you will be much more susceptible to those deceptions.

Unfortunately, the system of this world is designed to focus on selfish gain; That your life should reflect those impulsive reactions by satisfying your uncontrolled desires.

The more difficult but most rewarding pursuit is an intentional thought-out drive for a life full of doing the right things even when nobody is watching; Without seeking a reward or compensation.

Rise above the status quo to follow your primal instincts and live the life your intentions tell you you're already living.

Don't fake life...

live it with a developed conscience.

The baggage of your past,

does not belong in
the suitcase of your future.

Your feelings and emotions were given to you as a gift to live life with and you have complete control over them, so if they have control over you, the cart has rolled past in front of the horse.

If you let your feelings or emotions take the lead, they will almost always be negative and try to pull you down. Take control over them and choose which ones you want to experience.

More than likely the way you automatically respond is nothing more than a bad habit and habits can be kicked to the curb.

Create new, better, and more positive habits, but be aware… your ego will fight you with the chains that have had you bound to the same old routine and tell you that you can't change or it's too late for you.

There are ALWAYS choices to pull from; Just create for yourself which ones you want... THEN OWN IT!

~

Be yourself...

Because... If you think about it, it's none of your business what people think of you.

But... If you have to choose, think about this...

Some think that you are everything and some think you're nothing!

So choose to believe those who think the world of you because what they see is far more important than those who think nothing of you.

Those who think nothing of you… also think nothing of themselves.

Why would you want to believe anything coming from those who possess nothing but emptiness?

~

If your internal "happy" is affected by your external circumstances,
then you're not really happy!

~

It's impossible to get offended by what people say and do
if you give up trying to control what people say and do.

You be you and let them be them. It really is pretty simple…
Now go live life freely!

~

You are not your occupation, you are not your mistakes,
you are not your body shape, you are not an opinion of others,
you are not a color, you are not what you own
or how much money you have…

You are a one-of-a-kind soul that has been hand-made
by the Creator of the universe who does not
make mistakes. You have purpose, worth, beauty, strength,
talent, and wisdom that only you possess.

Breathe deep, smile, and just know that you are loved.
Believe/Trust that He is in control. Tomorrow is a new day.

~

Stop defining yourself by man-made words like:
personality, defect, diagnosis, disorder, looks, shape, weight,
skinny, fat, shy, and every other worthless word
that causes you to think less of what God Himself created you to be…

Fearfully and Wonderfully Made, the head and not the tail,
brave, bold, courageous, more than conquerors, just as you are…
Define yourself by the way God sees you, not man!

~

Relying totally on your feelings, in any situation, without backing them up with facts, is like a ship without any power or an anchor.

You can be blown around by the winds of assumption and have no reliable means of stability.

Even though the "feelings" themselves may be a fact to you, the reasons behind them could be something completely different, causing unnecessary and avoidable consequences:

Usually caused by always assuming you are "right" and without the need for correction on your part.

But a more reliable and stable way to maneuver your ship is to assume you are "wrong" until you have all the facts from every reliable source.

Never avoid anything or anyone, if your assumptions are based solely on feelings generated by a one-sided event or story.

Even if that story is your own.

～

The Peace that you seek is not found from any source found here on earth, not in money, jobs, material possessions, people, entertainment, pleasure, etc.

It is found only in the Maker of all things, the One who can generate that peace far deeper than any earthly source could ever compare.

Not temporal peace but true, deep, unexplainable peace that pours over you in the middle of chaos, when everything seems to be spinning out of control.

To find and experience this peace, first, you must place your trust, your life in the hands of your Creator, and just LET GO. Let go of the cares and worries, opinions, control, possessions… Let Go and Trust.

~

Everybody has a story,
no matter how old or young they are.
Everybody is going through something.
It may be on the mountain top now or in the valley,
but each person has their struggles to deal with.

You know neither their story nor their struggles,
so always proceed with love, understanding and compassion.
You could very well be the strength they need to get through the day.

~

Don't be so dang hard on yourself. If you're not perfect...
Congratulations... neither is anyone else.
Stop trying to figure everything out...
You're not going to anyway.

Live as if you didn't have a care in the world and don't be afraid
to try something new. Let your hair down, take a chance,
risk something scary, and have faith in the unseen part of
not knowing how things will turn out.

~

Think about this:
Your intentions will cause you to think that you're
tremendously more righteous than you actually are.
Meaning, pipe down on your judgmental attitude toward others.

~

Your mood button is not directly connected to your
circumstance panel; your choice button is.
This translates to: You can still have a good day or a joyful attitude
while your circumstances are simultaneously throwing
a fist full of kitty litter into your ice cream.

~

Everyone has to deal with their own struggles and everyone has a past... Your struggle is unique but you're not alone.

You have different circumstances, but you're not the only one going through them.

It's up to you to realize you have the power inside you to change your focus from MY problems to OUR problems and go through life as a team instead of as an isolated individual.

Don't find others to just commiserate with, but find others to hold and be held accountable to change for the better.

Your weakness is someone's strength.

Your strength is someone's weakness.

Thinking you're alone will cause you to feel sorry for yourself and feeling sorry for yourself will only drive you deeper into despair. Isolation breeds weakness, disparity, self-pity, and a loss of the will to live.

Unity breeds strength, compassion, selfless ambitions, and a will to live.

There is a spectrum of good and evil, positive and negative, right and wrong. Each are beckoning you for dominance.

Fight for the place you want to occupy and seek that community.

One way will always lead to death and the other side of that spectrum will always lead to life.

You know which is which...

Choose wisely.

~

Tell those negative thoughts and the demeaning self-talk to shut up...
Then git on about your day with the confidence of a swamp croc.

~

Rejection... Is neither an excuse nor a reason to give up!

~

We're all like a big bag of M&M's...
We all have different colored outer candy shells, but
on the inside, we're all filled with awesome chocolate.

So if you're judging someone by their candy shell
and not by the character of their chocolate filling,
then that's called being selfishly biased toward your own
empty prejudice preference for a shade of melatonin
that was assigned at birth.
It doesn't make sense when we all bleed the color of love.

~

If there's something you don't like about someone...
it's coming from an expectation you have for them.
In other words...
You'll like and get along with a whole lot more people
if you let them be them without any judgment attached.

~

Don't be misled by this subtle conditioning of language.

For instance,
the words "your opinion" are being replaced by "your truth"
as an attempt to water down the meaning of truth.
Truth DOES NOT change just because your mind changes.
There is either truth or opinion. Not both!

~

Self Righteousness says…

I'm already good enough, there is no need to change.

Self-righteous will always compare themselves to those who they deem to be more evil or worse off than they are so they can justify their behavior as being good.

Nothing they do is ever wrong because to them, there is someone else that does much worse things.

Stability says…

I have an anchor point source of perfection to strive towards so when I have a question, I can compare myself to the source... which will always come up short, but will compel you to keep moving forward in your walk to do better and be better.

Not to be mistaken for insecurity and an "I'll never be good enough to reach that standard so why try" attitude but an "I can always do better" standard to continually push you in a direction away from stagnant complacency.

This will spark a self-defined moral compass and a watered-down version of perfection, which in a way falls into the first category of self-righteousness.

So when there is a question on your self-defined moral structure…
Ask yourself this…

If I take a feeling, emotion, thought, action, etc. to the furthest side of the spectrum of perfection,

Does it line up to as close as what I am capable of doing?

And if I can do better... do it! Never settle for good enough.

~

Talk to people now,
as if you were reading your speech at their funeral.

~

People are seeking change without the willingness
to listen to the necessary truth to achieve it.
To embrace the new, you must let go of the old.

The change will never come in the same familiar
or comfortable package that you're used to getting.

The only pathway to positive, lasting change
is through discomfort, unfamiliar, uneasy, and
painful feelings of resistance.

Instead of looking at whatever negative circumstances
you're going through as a "bad" thing and fighting against it...

Consider it to be a "good" thing and learn
what it is that it is trying to teach you.

~

Sometimes what you feel like doing
isn't always what you should be doing.

~

A claim to believe in God doesn't necessarily render a devoted
commitment to the superior ways of the creator of the universe.
Because let's face it... to some people,
pizza is god, religion is god, self is god,
material possessions, movie/rock stars,
Or any other "surface happy nouns." Don't be fooled by the cheap
knock offs; they will never satisfy the deepest meanings in this life.

~

Think Positive

Thinking positive doesn't mean you don't still have negative thoughts, it just means you choose to think positive despite the negative.

You still have bad days, still have to deal with jerks, still don't feel like getting out of bed, still not a big fan of working at a job, still have to cope with things not working right or breaking down...

You just take a deep breath, accept it for what it is, and choose to push down the urge to complain, get angry, or stress out beyond your external control.

It means you develop the ability to take control of your actions and reactions instead of letting them control you.

On a side note...

(FACT)
Constant negativity causes physical and mental issues, So if you have the choice to either pick negativity and a slow death, or pick positivity with the benefits of not only being happier but feeling better about yourself,... wouldn't you want to experience the better side of life?

Yes, it's going to take work, but how much work did it take to get where you're at now?

You can and will do this, but don't do it alone...

And never give up.

~

Always choose to be the person that you want to be around.

~

Don't be deceived by
your intentions...

They will cause you to judge others
for also doing what you do.

~

If you breathe toxic air into your lungs, you damage your physical health. The more you breathe the worse it gets.

The same with "breathing" toxic thoughts into your brain.

Like negative self-talk, focusing on things to complain about, hateful projections on others, etc. the more you let in, the worse it gets for your mental health.

~

Divorce your imagination from your negative perceptions and marry your imagination to your positive perceptions.

Our perception of reality is heavily influenced by our imagination. If we are prone to gravitate towards the negative side of that spectrum our imagination can cripple us into believing the worst-case scenarios. Then, unfortunately, that belief will cause us to generate fear and ultimately every negative emotion that goes with it... stress, anxiety, worry, fear, dread, sadness, and eventually to a state of depression and the spiral downward into the loss of the very will to live, or death,

But...

If you choose to develop a more positive outlook on life, REGARDLESS OF YOUR CIRCUMSTANCES, you can imagine yourself in the best-case scenarios which will cause you to generate a sense of confidence.

Then from there the positive emotions that stem from that belief... peace, joy, love, excitement, contentment, freedom and so on, will lift you upwards and produce for yourself this gift of life everyone seeks to find.

The absolute best version of "YOU," is waiting on the other side of all the fears you keep avoiding.

~

If you're an unhappy person...

I would wager a considerable amount of potatoes
that you are an ungrateful person also.

The two walk on the beach hand in hand and deceive you,
while the sand is still fresh on your toes,
into believing that happiness comes BEFORE gratefulness
when, in fact, it's the contrary.

~

As long as your residence is still above the ground,
it is not too late to change your direction!

It is within your capacity to think
that you hold your potential future.

If you don't like the way your life is going,
then change your thoughts.

~

Excuses are False Reasons,
False Reasons are Deceptions,
Deceptions lead to Death either
mentally, spiritually, or physically.

So, in essence, every time you make an **excuse** to "do or not do,"
you are speaking death into your personal existence.
TODAY is the best day to change that !!!!!

~

If lies and corruption are your life, then
truth and the people who speak it are your enemies.

~

That nagging torment that claws at your insides, is the you that is trapped in your past, longing for the you that seeks to conquer your future!

In comparison...

A painful tooth will become infected, cause an abscess, and eventually rot. Then it will spread to the surrounding areas and may cause many other painful ailments or even death.

It's the same way with inner turmoil and mental issues, don't try to self-medicate for the purpose of drowning the inner torment, because in doing so, you will also drown your future self with it.

Your negative circumstances (pain) speak to you for your own good, not to wreck you or prevent your progress, but as a means to advance yourself into a better you... Fight it and reveal a bitter you.

Your bitterness and resentment are suppressed inner messages that need to be spoken. Let it out and say what you have to say. Speak your piece but make sure your piece is the truth.

Fix your pain before it spreads.

～

We all have our reasons why we either do or don't do or say something. We all have our demons to face and fight. Just know that a smile hides many struggles and pain.

We don't know what someone is going through on the inside. Stop judging why someone else does things the way we wouldn't or why others won't do what we would.

We all tend to judge ourselves with the overly-padded justifications of unrealistic intention and others by the harsh ridged actual reality of their actions.

We would all do well to reverse those sentences before we slam the gavel of self-righteousness.

~

Question...
Would it make more sense to teach one person
to NOT be offended by anything…
or to teach everyone on earth what NOT to do or say
to offend that one person?

Truth... Being offended by ANYTHING
is an excuse to blame OTHERS for YOUR behavior.

~

If you never challenge what you believe,
you will never find out why you believe what you believe.

~

Change your excuses into challenges!

~

What you believe, is what you live. What you live
reinforces your beliefs. Change what you choose to believe
and change the world you live in.

~

"Life and Death are in the power of the tongue."
What you speak to yourself in your thoughts
has the power to either breathe life into a hopeless existence,
or drive it deeper into despair.

~

You won't learn anything if you think you're always right.

~

Getting your feelings hurt by the truths
that you don't want to hear is not hate speech.

~

Whatever category you place yourself in, as far as identity, you are placing another brick in the wall of division. White, black, male, female, rich, poor, vaccinated, un-vaccinated, republican, democrat, geographical location, job title, employee, employer,... you get the picture.

You may be a part of each as a description but none are an identity to claim as who you are at the core.

We are all imperfect people in an imperfect world just trying to live as we see fit, to do the best we can with what we have.

If you feel that you are any better than someone else in the opposite category just because you believe different, You, my friend, are in denial of your capacity to fill the very same shoes that you condemn.

Open your blinded eyes, admit that you are wrong, see things from another point of view, and find out why you keep making the same mistakes.

Be aware of what you habitually think of and how you act... if you wouldn't like someone else acting as you do... fix it.

Point the finger at yourself instead of shifting the blame.

Stop judging yourself by your perfect intentions and others by their imperfect actions, because they are, in all actuality, one and the same.

~

The more you feed your anger and hatred, the more you will find to feast on.

It will slowly take control until it becomes a part of you...

Be aware of your choices; they become your reality...

Life gives you what you focus on.

~

When the name-calling and useless profanities begin,
the intelligent conversation ends.

~

You can lead a human to knowledge,
but you can't make'em think!

~

You can kill the message and the messenger,
but you can't kill the truth.

~

Has anything bad happened to you?
I know... stupid question, but what have you done with it?

1) Let it get the best of you and spend a huge part of your life
being defeated by what happened by living in the past?
Or
2) Get back on the horse and conquer the day with
confidence, vision, and purpose?

One has a victim mentality and the other is a victor.
Not perfect, but willing to keep moving forward
through every opportunity to learn, which some call failure.

~

Happiness does not depend on
anything going the way you want it to
or getting what you want...

It simply depends on the choice you make to be happy.

Regardless...

~

A massive voluntary change in yourself brings with it an equal involuntary change in those around you.
They will either embrace who you are becoming with open arms and encouragement to be the better you, or they will fight against your change because it means that they might have to change also.

Change is a scary thing for those who have grown accustomed to the comfort zone.

During any transformation, however, there is an adjustment period that can get ugly due to over-or-under-compensation in the process. Sometimes you hit your mark, sometimes you fall short, but, eventually, things will reach an equilibrium.

Those who want to support your desire to always strive to become a better person will be patient, understanding along your journey, and want to come with you. Others will either fight to keep you the same or sever whatever ties they have with you.

These are natural steps in the process because not everyone is on the same journey as you.
Let things play out the way they play out. Those who are supposed to be in your life will still be there for every level of transformation that you achieve.

~

You will eliminate every argument in your life when you eliminate the need to give your point of view as fact.

Switch to a curious stance in your conversations and actually listen to others' views by wanting to know how they came to their understanding.

Promote unity by understanding, even if you disagree. You can understand and disagree at the same time.
Don't fall for the separation and disunity tactics of mainstream media outlets; they are no longer a reliable source of non-biased journalism.

~

A day early and a dollar more!

~

Life is meant to enjoy the things you already have,
not complain about the things you don't.

Just live!!!

~

Did You Know?
That just one wrong thought leads to a wrong action
which eventually turns into a wrong habit
then ultimately into a wrong lifestyle.

The result of a life that isn't in harmony
with truth is discomfort.

This presents itself as anger, frustration,
depression, anxiety, worries, stress and so on…

With that in mind… IF your thinking is wrong,
wouldn't you want to know it so you could fix it?

Resulting in a balanced life of peace, joy, love,
thankfulness, and enjoying life.

~

Remember this next Thanksgiving...
Practice safe stuffing.

~

Freedom from your inner pain is on the other side of your
self-made prison built by the bricks of negative thoughts.

~

Sometimes trying to find the reasoning behind life's little so-called inconsistencies are a feat in itself, when other times the answers are self-evident.

The ones that perplex us are the ones that keep us on a never-ending rat wheel until, or if, we ever find the reasoning behind it all.

Are some things worth trying to find the hidden meaning to, if there is a hidden meaning?

The questions like… why did they have to go before their time?
Or why such a painful breakup, or the loss of a job, and so on.

Maybe they didn't go before their time, but rather AT their time or maybe a breakup was because it wasn't supposed to be in the first place or the end of a job was the beginning of a new career and all we have to learn is acceptance.

Sometimes we never do find the concrete answers to the difficult questions of life, but I can tell you this…

Whatever you dwell on is the direction you head.

If that's the past then that is where you'll live; if it's the future then that is where you'll live.

The past is full of regrets and the future is full of worries, so the only real way to live is in each present moment.

Yes, learn from the past because that is its purpose, and plan for the future, but don't forget to cherish the moments and live right here and right now.

~

QUESTION:

Which do you have
the power to change,
The Past or The Future?

Let the answer be what you put
all your heart into today,

and don't spend one more second
on the other!

~

~

Mysteriously, your woes will leave when your complaints do…

~

You can't learn forgiveness without having someone to forgive.

Before you pass judgment, open up to the fact that
this could just be another opportunity to grow.

Pride is the lock that keeps us trapped in the prison
of unforgiveness. Let go and walk in freedom.

~

The Past...
A place to occasionally visit and recall lessons,
but not a place to unpack or take up residency.

There is a key to a future with your name on it, but you have to drop
off the keys of your past that keeps your name on the deed.

Letting go of your past doesn't mean letting go of memories,
it just means you have made up your mind to open the next door
without physically bringing them with you,
so you can make room for new memories.

The only door that is available and remains open is called
your future. Live there and always face that door.
Every time you check the door to your past,
it is, and always will remain locked.

~

We are in an age where people would rather force everyone on the
planet to cater to their insecurities so they don't **get** offended,
instead of fixing their insecurities so they no longer will **be** offended.

~

~

Don't ever let someone or something pull you away from the road
you know you're supposed to be on. Guard your mind and never
rely on your ever-changing feelings over the truth.

~

Whatever we pray for, God gives us: maybe
through experiencing whatever it takes to get us there,
as long as it aligns with His will.

Very rarely is it a direct path to the end result.
So instead of praying for the end result,
pray for the strength and wisdom to arrive there
through whatever path it takes.

~

The simple skinny... Happiness hinges on gratitude.
If you aren't happy, you aren't thankful.

~

Change the way you see externally
to change the way you feel internally.

~

If you have to be in control of everything
in your life or in your relationships...
then you're not in control of anything.

~

Confidence is a practice,
not something that just shows up one day.

You'll never be ready to start anything that requires it,
So take the first step and just get started.

~

~

The faith of a grain of a mustard seed can move mountains…
So conversely... the doubt of that same grain can also cause
those mountains to overshadow your world.

So don't doubt...
Just believe! Both are decisions on your part.

~

Navigating throughout the day
with your feelings dictating your emotional stability
is like letting the waves steer your ship across the ocean.

Grab the rudder wheel and rely on intentional responsive action
not automatically reacting out of triggered habitual programming.

~

The sun is always shining
even though sometimes you can't see it.
Just like sometimes you have to still be thankful
even though you're not experiencing anything yet.

Live by faith and not those ever-changing, unreliable feelings.

~

Pure gold first goes through a process of refinement
to get rid of the impurities. When they rise to the surface,
they are removed to transform it into a more pure state.

Our negative reactions to adverse circumstances are the
impurities in us. When we negatively react to those situations,
remove the reactions to refine yourself into a more pure state.

Let them refine us into being better, not bitter.

~

~

There is a deceptive illusion that you have to mimic
your feelings by acting them out in your attitude and behavior...
It's a lie...
feelings are the horses and your attitude is the cart.
Don't put the cart before the horse.

~

Bad habits can come in many forms; negativity is one of them.
Practice being grateful until that is your new habit.

~

Make "now" the time you change... Try this:
Instead of telling people everything wrong in your life
and the things you don't like about it... start telling them
everything that is right and what you do like about it.

~

If you're constantly seeking external sources for reassurance UNTIL
you get through something,
you will continue to seek that form of reassurance.

But if you practice your own internal reassurance for self-confidence,
YOU will be what it takes TO get through it.

Seeking reassurance from **outside** of you is a habitual circle
that won't end until you find it **within** yourself.

Yes, take reassurance whenever it externally presents itself, but use it
to add to your confidence, not as a pacifier.

~

Not addressing an issue because you think the worst, will never end in
resolve. Always pursue your assumptions until they turn into facts.

~

~

If your experience with religion/church is generating any form of
obligation as opposed to appreciation, then you should reconsider
the position you are committing yourself to.
Never choose religion over God.

~

When you grasp the fact that your beliefs are what dictate
your life, then you will be able to walk through
many more doors of opportunity.

~

The Source of life is the best starting point for all your woes.

~

YOUR outcomes revolve around YOUR choices.
Anger, stress, anxiety, worry, fear, hatred, impatience,
arrogance, worthlessness, and ugliness…
ARE ALL CHOICES
that trigger a feeling or emotion that creates a
negative imbalance to the original divine design.
Those TAKE FROM your life.
Choose love, peace, joy, patience, trust, humility, beauty,
worth, and every other feeling or emotion that promote positivity
and ADD TO your life.

No matter what you're "feeling" at the time.
Feelings DO NOT dictate your thoughts or actions,
unless you choose them to do so.

~

Whatever you're going through,
there's always a reason to not give up.
FIND IT!

~

~

If you're always looking at what is wrong in your life,
you'll never see what is right in it.

Your focus is your future.

~

Smile...
It's hard to be in a bad mood if you're smiling.

~

Plug into nature, the ultimate recharging station.

~

We were designed to thrive with a Divine nature.
The more we align ourselves to the source of all life,
the more our reflection of Him radiates in our life
and the more life makes sense.
We are then free to be who we were created to be...
Divinely designed souls full of purpose...
love, joy, peace, compassion, gratitude, mercy,
freedom, and active hope.

~

Nature has a way of taking on some pretty unique shapes
due to some past circumstantial adversities
that forced them out of the "normal" expected growth.

Has some adversity in your past thrown you
out of the expected "normal" and changed your life?

Instead of thinking that you're different, in a bad way,
embrace it as being Unique and choose to live this life
to its fullest potential inside of who you are right now.

~

~

Make Happy Your Habit!

~

Thoughts follow a certain path
just like a train follows a certain track.
If it never changes, you will always end up in the same place.

If your switch track is set along the way
to a specific destination and that destination
is a place you would rather not end up,
then consult with the track master to change
the switch track to the destination you prefer.

That track master… is you!

~

The only obstacles between you and the life you dream of
are the obstacles between your ears.

Your thoughts are more destructive to your life
then the circumstances you give that power to.

When you focus on the "things" that are outside of your mind,
the things on the inside follow suit…
Reverse that process and focus more on
your internal life to influence the external.

~

Don't ever invite failure to your party;
it's one of those guests that will ruin the ending.

If it shows up uninvited…
don't entertain it, ignore it until it goes away.

~

~

You only get angry at those **you** try to control.
You only get offended by those you **let** control you,
and a mixture of both.

~

Every action you take, every thought you think,
every direction you go,
are decisions you made to choose either right or wrong,
good or evil, positive or negative, perfection or perversion...
and those choices then turn into your lifestyle,
which results in whatever consequences you experience in life.

If you choose to be negative, then you will experience negative
consequences. If you choose to be positive, then you will experience
positive circumstances.

~

If you're miserable... you're selfish.
Your life is all about you and what you want, but don't have;
which means that your focus is on lack.

You gain joy when you focus on what you already have
and are truly grateful for it.
Your mindset is to give and not get, because you live in abundance.

So if you're struggling with life, you struggle with mindset.

~

Fixing your mind is better than altering it... And much cheaper too.
If you spend as much on investing in yourself
as you spend on the substances you use to cope with life,
starting now, next year you will be a completely different
and a much better version of you.

~

~

The only way to true wisdom
is to let go of the deception that you are always right.

~

The mood doesn't dictate attitude; attitude dictates mood!
If you want to be in a good mood, focus on your attitude.

~

You!
The only person that's standing in your way!

~

Relying on circumstances to dictate your happiness,
is like expecting a roller coaster to deliver
a straight flat ride... It will never happen and will always
bring you right back to where you started.
It's not what it was designed for.

Let circumstances shape you into a consistently
joyful person regardless of your preferences.
Enjoy the ride, wherever it takes you.

~

Everyone can treat someone else nicely
that also treats them nice...
But if you treat someone badly because they treat you bad,
are you not acting in the same way that you are opposed to?

Be different and treat everyone nicely
regardless of how they treat you.

Be an example of Love.
Not a mirror of Hatred.

~

~

You will find what is right
when you're open to being wrong.

You will only learn
when you're ready to listen.

~

~

Can and Can't

Both are word choices that will lead you to your beliefs.
The one you choose is the one that wins... Every time.

So choose that you can, and then believe it to be so.

~

If you pursue the absolute core function of
unconditional love within yourself towards others,
you will find a depth of life
that cannot be equaled in any other pursuit.

Look outside of yourself to find Life… Then live it to the fullest.

~

I'd rather have the wind knocked out of me
and be stopped dead in my tracks by the truth
than to be deceptively happy and strung along with a lie.

Fight to keep the Truth alive
by living within its boundaries at all costs.

~

Your levels of anger, stress, anxiety, fear, depression,
and so on are a reflection in direct proportion
to your desire for external control.

Give up on trying to manipulate your surroundings
to always go your way (people or situations)
and that list of negative reactions will disappear from your life.

Control your reactions, not your circumstances.

~

~

Truth spoken with love and understanding
will open more ears than aggressive opinions.

~

If you must be guilty of something...
Be guilty of Loving too much.

~

Our perceptions are not always grounded in reality.

Our beliefs are based on our perceptions.

Let this sink in for a few minutes…

If your perceptions are skewed,
your reality is skewed and
you are living inside of an altered reality
full of false beliefs...

If you are wrong in your beliefs,
wouldn't you want to know the truth
so that you can fix it and start living inside reality?

If you always think you're right,
you'll never learn anything new.

~

Your road to success and greatness
is straight through the path of adversity.

Persevere with gratitude and determination
and you will make it.

~

~

Fear is nothing more than an illusion
that keeps you on the wrong side of a thin veil
that reveals your destiny.

~

Nobody sees the demons that hide
just behind the smile, unless that smile is yours.
When they make their way out,
it's usually taken as harsh behavior behind the cold stare of pain.

The bitter chains of loneliness can overtake someone
even in a crowd. So, in a world filled with demons,
be the angel that breaks the darkness with a smile and a kind word.
Breathe life back into a wounded soul.

~

Absolute truth does not diminish
within your inability to recognize it.

~

If you've had a crappy day, month, year, life, etc.,
it's because you have chosen to believe that!
What you choose to believe has nothing to do with your
circumstances, and everything to do with your frame of mind.

It is completely possible to have
100% chaos going on around you,
and simultaneously have 100% peace of mind on the inside.

~

Trust in The God of the universe, NOT in a universal god.

The difference is eternal.

~

Bite Size

~

Trade the things that waste your time for the things
that will make a difference in your life.
Example:
Negative thoughts for Positive thoughts.
Past hurts for Future goals.
T.V. (dead thinking) for a book. (stimulate the brain)
Potato chips for Celery sticks
Sitting in front of Facebook for a brisk walk.
Thinking about doing something for actually doing it.
I Can't for I Can
Etc...
Add to the list, share one trade-off for the Other...

~

If your reason for living is attached to anything
that can cease to exist at any moment...
you have already set yourself up for disappointment and failure.

~

Instead of trying to scare people out of hell,
Try loving them into Heaven.

~

Sometimes we fight so hard to be who we are...
without even knowing yet... who we are...

Find your identity in the One who gave you
the breath of life, and you will find you.

Nothing this world has to offer will ever satisfy
the deep longings that burn within your soul.
Search within your heart,
not in the external temporary desires of the carnal flesh.

~

~

Religion and God
are two completely different entities.
Give to Caesar what is Caesar's and to God what is God's.

~

Keep your head above the sea of negativity.
Don't let the world's system of lies, manipulation, control,
and greed pull you under. If someone chooses to lie about you
or steal from you... Immediately forgive them for your sake,
accept your losses, let go and don't give them
another chance to do it again.

A grudge will only pull you down; it does nothing to them.

There is only freedom waiting for you in the release of material
possessions, and a prison where you surround yourself
with the bars of "things" or take from others through your
deceptive justifications driven by "selfishness."

If you find yourself in the trap of wanting to fill "your" barns
with things that will only rot or rust, the weight on your shoulders
will only increase with every ounce of "want"
that flows out of your desires.

~

Be careful so that when you open your mouth,
your religion doesn't fall out.

~

If your "auto-response" to life tends
to gravitate toward the negative side of things...

Cast your net over the other side of the boat.

~

Bite Size

~

Life is such a blessing!
Stop wasting your time on the pursuit of money or material
gain; all of it starts out shiny and attractive,
but eventually rusts or rots.

Start spending your time on adventures, memories with friends
and family, and living this gift of life to the fullest capacity.

Live free without worry, stress, or complaining.
Be thankful for everything; yes, even the bad, because if you
put that into practice, you will find that even the
"perceived" bad in your life is for a better purpose that turns out
good. Complaining only leads to more complaining, let go and live!

~

If you don't believe in a higher power that created every living thing,
simply because you're not sure that He's real,
maybe it's time you call to clean out your SKEPTIC tank.

~

Don't let your differences be your division.

Everyone has something special to bring to the table.
We are all a diverse melting pot of likes, interests, feelings,
goals, ambitions, and talents, etc., so when we meet someone
or already know someone that's different from us,
make that your excuse to learn from
or better yourself through them,
instead of letting it separate you from them
or look down on them for being different.

Let's face it,
they are looking at you for being different too.

~

~

You live what you believe…
What you believe was first a decision,
either by you or someone you learned from…
Your decisions are nothing more than choices…
Choose what you decide to believe…

Choose Life - Then Live it.
With as much confidence and emotion as you can muster.

~

Go outside and blaze some trails.
Breathe deep and love life no matter what it throws at you.

~

The wealthy and the poor have achieved what they have
through the same process of thoughts.

One chooses to push past adversity,
obstacles, comfort, opposition,
negative feedback, and every other circumstance
of resistance that stands in front of them.

The other has an excuse for each.

~

The difference between Win or Lose is the attitude of Do or Try.

~

PERSISTENCE
The ability to try one more time… Multiple times…
Until you have achieved what you've set out to achieve.

NEVER GIVE UP!

~

~

Find Reasons not to give up.
Break the habit of thinking that feelings, emotions, fears,
worries, skepticism, anxieties, or stresses are at all
legitimate reasons to stop or give up on anything.

~

The Heart of the matter.
If you are trying to change anything that someone is doing
to cause harm to people or the environment without first
changing their heart, you are wasting your time.

~

Keep Your Why in The Way.
Know Why you do what you do
and your DO will eventually get done.

~

This is your day.
Do with it what you will.

~

Your self worth isn't determined by anybody but you.
Choose your worth.

Negative emotions and demeaning self-talk
are just as habitual as any other bad habit.

Your triggered reactions to any given circumstance can be
reprogrammed by first being aware that your thinking
has been hijacked by influences before you had a choice.

Self-worth is NOW your choice.
Choose Life

~

~

Truth is the foundation in which you should find your way,
Not the ever-changing emotions and feelings
that keep you crashing like the waves on the shore.

Don't try to find yourself by changing the truth…
Find the truth to change yourself.

~

The habits you make in your mind through thoughts
are the habits that will come alive through your actions
to eventually become your reality.

100% of all inner struggles that you face,
are either won or lost on the battlefield of the mind.

~

Confidence is a Decision…
Not a feeling!

Don't wait until you "feel" confident before you do
whatever you want to do that you believe needs confidence.
The only thing you need is action…
Do it regardless of your feelings.
It takes practice like everything else.

~

If you're not being a part of the solution,
You're being a part of the problem.

Standing still is moving backwards.
If you know something is wrong and don't act on it,
it's not doing what you know to be right
which essentially is doing the wrong thing.

~

~

Don't ever let your
PAST encounters

Dictate your
FUTURE endeavors.

~

~

Self-righteous... Pointing out everyone else's faults while ignoring your own. So... Complain about your own issues more than anyone elses. That way you'll get sick of hearing yourself complain and do something about it.

~

Without suffering, there is no growth. So before you try and go around, avoid, or drown out your supposed inconveniences, open up to the possibility that they just might be trying to tell you something that will bring you to the place you have been wanting to go all along... It just happens to be on the other side of your suffering. Buckle up, set your face like a flint and go straight through the middle with the determination of a third monkey on the ramp to Noah's Ark.

~

The self-righteous ego is blind to its own prideful arrogance.

~

Love like there's no tomorrow.

~

Embrace your trials and come out the other side on top. If you get angry, complain, and fight your trials you will continue to repeat them. Be thankful for everything in your life, it has a purpose for good.

~

The door God has closed cannot be opened! The door He opens, cannot be closed!

~

Some have mistaken being belligerent, loud-mouthed, in your face, and arrogant as... being yourself.

~

When all the selfishness, materialism,
expectations and control are purged,
you're left with pure intention.
Intentions and thoughts mingle into words and
actions that give way to habits and eventually into a lifestyle.

Like gold, intentionally put your thoughts through the crucible
to remove the dross (above list)
for a life disciplined enough to be an example.

~

Guilt
We all need an outlet to release our guilt.
And the best way to do that permanently,
from this point forward,
is to live a life that doesn't generate it.

Live a pure life my friends;
no judgment, lies, or deception.
Be kind and courteous, be fair, don't be selfish,
see things through others' eyes, be understanding,
and don't talk about others: You get the picture.

~

The only difference between you and the people you put
on a pedestal are a few tiny bits of information,
which means that if you knew what they know,
you could be where they are.

Never underestimate the power of learning...
and don't stop at just learning the knowledge part,
put it into action by breathing life into that knowledge.

~

SUMMARY

If I were to boil everything down to a small bullet list of the most important items I've learned throughout the years and emphasize the takeaway points I would suggest walking away with it would be as follows:

* First, be consciously aware of your automatic, reactionary, habitual, and negative behavior patterns so you can start the process of re-conditioning them into a more intentional response to adversities in a positive light.

* Accepting things for what they are with a good attitude and the ability to calmly respond to circumstances with, "It happened, now what?" Then find a solution to move forward in the most productive way possible.

* Give up all external control, such as unrealistic expectations, judgmental projections, stereotyping, looking at others as beneath you, assumptions, and trying to dictate what people say, how they act, or what they do. You only have control over those things in yourself and how you respond to them.

* Always look at things as if you could be wrong so you can correct them, don't be afraid of accepting fault, be humble, and don't assume you know everything. Be open to advice and constructive criticism.

* Always try to understand viewpoints through the eyes of whomever you are speaking with, regardless if you agree with them or not. Converse with the intent to listen and understand, not to wait for them to stop talking so you can interject your opinions.

* Know that you have the power within yourself to make your life what you will, no one but you is responsible for the way your life turns out. Blaming others or any part of your life will only keep you stuck in a victim mindset.

* Master these skills and you will notice your arguments will either cease to exist or drastically reduce.

If these are not already a part of your daily routine, make it a lifelong goal to put this list into practice and your life will improve greatly.

Refer back to this page regularly
as a reminder for your mental health.

Much Love.

~ THANK YOU ~

Best of Luck, Many Blessings, and Much Love

If you've made it to this page, I just want to say—thank you. Truly.

Time is the most valuable thing we have, and the fact that you chose to spend some of it with my words means more than you know. Whether this book stirred something new in you, challenged your perspective, or simply gave you something to think about on a quiet afternoon ~ I am grateful that you came along for the journey.

If the content resonated with you in any way, I'd be honored if you took a few moments to head back to where you picked up this book and leave a star rating and an honest review.   *(Direct Amazon QR Code Above)*
Your words matter more than algorithms—reviews help future readers know if this book belongs in their hands too.

If you're the kind of person who enjoys chewing on life's deeper questions, and maybe even laughing a little while doing it, I'd love to stay connected. Come join the tribe of thinkers, soul-searchers, and dragon-sleighers—yes, they're real—by hopping on the newsletter.

No fluff. No spam. Just thought-provoking musings, first looks at new projects, and the occasional spark to brighten your day or ignite your mind.

You can join us at: www.rickbartrand.com (Your inbox deserves meaningful company.) Until next time ... Stay curious. Stay courageous. And never stop seeking the truth.

With much gratitude; ~ *Rick* ~

ABOUT THE AUTHOR

Rick is a truth-seeker and author who has spent decades charting the unexplored territories of the human spirit, faith, and freedom.

Born and raised in Michigan, Rick's love for the wild outdoors and quiet reflection has shaped a life devoted to uncovering timeless wisdom and sharing it with fellow authentic truth-seekers, soul warriors, and skeptics, ready to saddle dragons and ride.

From humble beginnings flipping burgers and working construction to serving his country as a U.S. Navy air-crewman on combat support helicopters, Rick's boots-on-the-ground life experience gives him raw authenticity you can feel on every page.

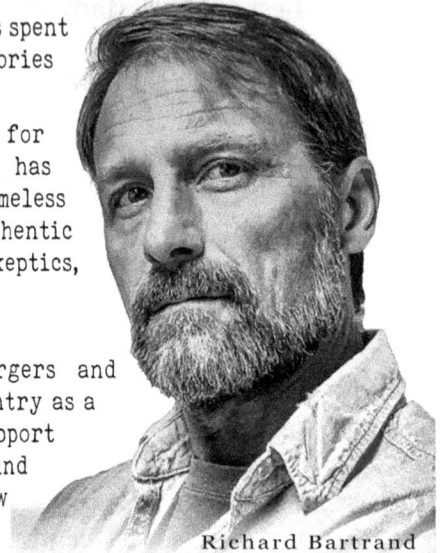

Richard Bartrand

He's a skilled handyman, an over-the-road truck driver, built businesses, and guided others as a thought coach, helping to reclaim inner strength and clarity.

But Rick's greatest adventure didn't come from the road or the sky, it came through a thorough analysis into self-mastery, spiritual awakening, and philosophical exploration. Over 20 years of journaling, seeking, and learning forged his voice as an author who doesn't offer fluff or feel-good clichés, but bold truths that challenge your thinking and ignite your soul.

When he's not writing, you'll find Rick capturing wildlife through a camera lens in the Michigan woods, or sharing stories beside the warm glow of a crackling campfire.

MORE BOOKS BY THIS AUTHOR

And more to come for those who dare to question, seek, and live fully awake.

PERSONAL DEVELOPMENT

BITE SIZE LIFE LESSONS
Modern-Day Proverbs * Volumes 1 & 2

BITE-SIZED REAL-WORLD WISDOM FOR EVERYDAY APPLICATIONS

From overcoming challenges to embracing change, this is your personal road-map to self-improvement, personal success, and a life of intention. Filled with practical insights, timeless wisdom, and real-world strategies, every page of Bite Size Life Lessons is designed to challenge your thinking and elevate your personal growth.

- Live with focused intention.

- Strengthen your mindset and self-awareness.

- Eye-opening revelations.

You're not just buying a book ...

you're investing in decades of practical wisdom that can shift your thinking for the better, one page at a time.

SPIRITUAL AWAKENING

SO... YOU THINK YOU'RE AN ATHEIST
Questions That Haunt The Soul

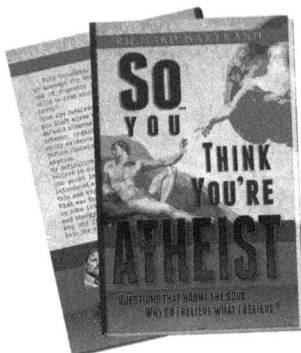

FINDING CLARITY IN BETWEEN DOGMA AND SKEPTICISM

Inside a world of conflicting beliefs and dogmatic worldviews, it often feels impossible to find answers. This is your guide to navigating these murky waters and uncovering the universal truths that lie between rigid doctrines and skeptical perspectives. Many find themselves trapped in the misconception that rejecting organized religion must automatically lead to atheism.

- Reflect deeply on your thoughts and beliefs.
- Convincing arguments don't always lead to facts.
- How logic can coexist with authentic faith

In an endless sea of worldviews ... This is your anchor buoy!

"The arduous battle through religion and atheism almost drove me insane... until I let go of both." This raw, honest journey is for those who dare to ask: *"What if there's more?"*

THOUGHT-PROVOKING

SMOKING THE PIPE OF CONTEMPLATION
Road To Revelation * Volume 1

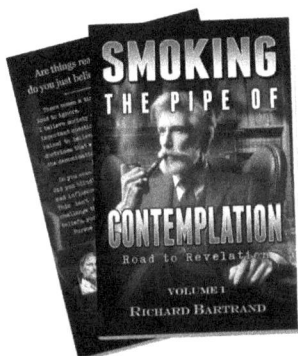

A PHILOSOPHICAL JOURNEY INTO THE ABYSS OF REFLECTIVE THOUGHT.

Have you unknowingly inherited a worldview crafted by those who came before you? This isn't about telling you what to believe—it's about exploring, deconstructing, and rediscovering truth through raw personal reflections, deep philosophical inquiries, and candid takes on modern controversies, it will push you into the crater of critical thinking, self-awareness, and reflective thought.

- A spark of curiosity and mindfulness.
- Mental clarity and emotional intelligence.
- Compelling perspectives on life's meaning.

Read with an open mind. Walk away with it sharpened.

If you're ready to question, to contemplate, and to uncover deeper truths, then this book is your invitation to fire up the Pipe of Contemplation.

PLANNING / ORGANIZATION

90-DAY GOAL PLANNER
Reach Your Intended Goals

TRACK YOUR DAILY / WEEKLY PROGRESS

3 - four-week daily planners plus one week to transition into your next 90-day list of goals.

A 30-day and a 60-day checkpoint to stay on track to reach your 90-day target.

Keep your next 3 months organized with this daily / weekly / monthly / quarterly production goal planner.

- Reach your intended goals.
- Track your daily / weekly progress.
- 30 & 60 Day Production Checkpoints

A written dream attached to a date becomes a goal.

Measure progress and add accountability, it becomes a plan.

Integrate it into your daily practice and it becomes a reality.

CHILDREN'S BOOK

THE ADVENTURES OF SUZIE Q AND HATTIE SNACKS
TWIN FLAMES

AN EVERYDAY QUEST TO FIND AND EXPLORE SOMETHING NEW.

Embark on a delightful journey with Suzie Q and Hattie Snacks as they explore the wonders of their everyday world.

This colorful and imaginative children's poem cartoon book invites young readers to tag along on the twins' playful adventures around the house.

- Playful, Fun, Joyful, and Adventurous.
- Big Bold Print
- Colorful Illustrations

Your children will enjoy following along on the adventures of Suzie Q and Hattie Snacks for many years to come, with its fun and creative, bright and happy pictures along with big bold print as they learn how to read.

CONTACT INFORMATION

WEB SITE
WWW.RICKBARTRAND.COM

AMAZON AUTHOR PAGE
WWW.AMAZON.COM/AUTHOR/RICHARDBARTRAND

The Social Con-nection

FACEBOOK
@RICKBARTRANDTHOUGHTCOACH

INSTAGRAM
@RB_THOUGHTCOACH

LINKEDIN
@RICKBARTRAND

YOUTUBE
@RB_THOUGHTCOACH

TWITTER (X)
@RICKBARTRAND

SEE YOU SOON!

www.ingramcontent.com/pod-product-compliance
Lightning Source LLC
Chambersburg PA
CBHW061959040426
42447CB00010B/1828